Welcome

LIFELAND

A COMPANION

Professor James Caspet

Published by Garamonde 2019

GARAMONDE

International distribution.
Copyright (Text and Covers) 2019.
The moral right of the author has been asserted.

All rights reserved. No part of this book may be reproduced or transmitted in any form or by any means, electronic or mechanical, including photocopying, recording or by any information storage and retrieval system, without prior knowledge and permission in writing from the author.

Production by Media Services

Part 1
Basic Stuff

The Universe
Gods
Humans
Dogs
Wine
Emotions
Ideas
Art & Expression
Landscape
Earth
Trees
People (Are Sheep)
Rituals
Power
Chocolate and Bread
Life
The Brain
Time
Death
The Past
The Future
Nothing

Part 2
Thinking

Why
How
Where
Other

Part 3
What Next

What to worry about

Why to not

Paths to take

Places to Avoid

Exercises

BONUS
Thoughts, Ideas
and Questions

Professor James Caspet has had an interest in Human Behaviour all of his academic life. As part of his studies he became happily married and had some lovely children whom he sees regularly in between his various postings.
His dogs are called Maximum and Minimum.

So let's begin.

First the disclaimer. If you bought this book thinking it may contain answers to all those things that have puzzled you for so long, then take it back immediately and ask for a refund.

I don't have answers. I have ideas. I have questions. So many questions. Mostly I have a fascination. About the curious and apparent fact that we exist.
Somewhere and somehow we arrived here.
I don't know where here is but it appears to be a mildly pleasant place in which various species including us have managed to survive in varying degrees of comfort or discomfort so far.
Whether this situation will continue or is merely temporary is a moot point.

Second disclaimer. This is not a highly researched textbook. It's a chat amongst friends around a table, a fire, a bar, at a beach, on top of a mountain.
Wherever you like to be for some earnest discussion.
As we all know, when chatting with friends in a relaxed atmosphere there can be some rather odd claims and declarations. And facts may be presented that could be challenged. Repetition and overlaps may occur as subjects are approached from different angles.
It's all part of the interaction of this group of sentient beings we have named humans.

So as one human to another. I hope you enjoy the following pages.
If you get annoyed, delighted or enriched then that is good.
Whatever happens, I will have enjoyed your company for a while and I hope we part friends.

James

The Universe

Imagine you're living on a grain of sand ....

Imagine you're living on a grain of sand on a very large beach. All your experience, all your knowledge, your concept of who you are, what you are and what it all means, has come from your explorations of your grain of sand and your observations from your grain of sand.
This very roughly equates to our own experience on planet earth. (Many will say my beach is too small.)

Apart from a few tentative steps toward some very close neighbours we have gained all our information, to date, from this method of looking outward and guessing what it's all about. No problem with that. It's the best we've got at the moment. How sure are we that what we surmise is correct or even close to an answer or a fact for that matter?
Well, a lot and a little.
With such incredibly limited resources and narrow view, we have managed to figure out quite a lot about how it all goes together.
The trap is to know which bits are right, which bits are entirely wrong and which are open to greater scrutiny.

Any examination of our history will show examples of welded on facts that our forebears believed without question, that have since been proved to be completely wrong.
One problem we have is living on a world where everything has a beginning and an end, while trying to come to terms with the possibility that the universe -
1. Was always there.
2. Suddenly just happened.
3. Is teeming with life.
4. Is devoid of life.
(Except for us. Are we some hideous malfunction? A cancer of sorts.)
5. Is all an illusion.
6. Is part of some larger structure.
(Are our celestial bodies merely the other atoms in a giant's kitchen table leg?)

7. Is endless.
Better stop. This list could be much longer.
How big is the universe? Somebody pointed out that some starlight visible in our night sky may be from stars that have come into being, lived and died while their light was travelling to us. One day we'll look up and they just won't be there anymore. Or they may slowly fade. Anyway, that's big.
What is the universe? Of course, nobody on planet earth knows. It's just there. Ask an astrophysicist or a radio astronomer and you'll get an answer. Whether it will be a particularly satisfying answer or one that you can tick off as 'solved' is highly unlikely.
Many learned men have written endless texts hypothesising all sorts of reasons for and about the universe and to be fair, we might as well discuss the whole thing, rather than just ignore it and say we don't know. But we don't.
(See next chapter.)

What to do? What can you do about the universe?
Well, be aware that it's out there and whether we like it or not, we appear to be in it.
I said it's big, before. It's vast. In fact 'vast' is an inadequate word for it. Vast is used to describe the Amazon rainforest of the Russian steppes but something where your nearest solar system neighbour is many light years away, is a whole new concept of vast. Feel free to invent new non-scietific words for how big the universe is and the distances between things in the universe.

On a more earthly, doable scale.
Take yourself away from any artificial lights, to some dark and open part of the country, on a clear night. Lay down on the ground and look up. You may be shocked and say, "Hey, I've never noticed that before."
The massive array of things to see in the cosmos. For those who have never 'noticed' the universe before it can be a little daunting. You may feel that you're in a tiny boat on 'vast' ocean but be calmed by the knowledge that earth has

been here for billions of years and (as far as we can tell) there's a lot of life in the ol' girl yet. (Unless there's a massive meteor we've failed to notice.)

The universe (must be the greatest 'collective' noun of all time) is a wondrous thing.
Admire it, love it, be in awe of it, sit around with a few people and discuss it, enjoy it but most of all be proud of yourself. You're part of it.

Gods

What do you do when you don't understand ....

What do you do when you don't understand? It seems you create a god. Some supernatural being that neatly plugs up all the holes in your knowledge and allows you to invest your entity with whatever fantastic powers and virtues you feel are necessary to make you feel comfortable.
From the simple carved statue in some native village to the grand, ornate edifices of the west and the east, we've all been at it from the moment we had some spare time and were able to communicate.

Examined carefully, without prejudice, it appears that there is an unspoken but obvious underlying reason for wanting to create gods and then attach much ceremony and a whole swag of rules and regulations to said, god. It is power!

I imagine that the first god was probably created by chance. There's always some person in any collection of people who has a talent for spinning a yarn. Capturing people's attention with much talk and the examination of ideas.
In contemporary society these people become politicians or car salesmen but back in ancient times, around our campfire, (a fire built because we are afraid of the dark and what terrors it might enshroud) they offered a unique chance.
Our silver-tongued entrepreneur decides to expand his nightly ramblings with some little more outrageous imaginings. Aware of his fellows timidity when it comes to the dark he introduces a super being, one who will protect and guide them when they are troubled or scared. Amazed at how readily the gathering accept his story and this being, he makes the leap that all god creators make.
"I (insert name here) am (insert new god's name here) emissary. If you follow my word and obey my commands (this god) will look kindly upon you and protect you."
They readily agree. In one simple move, he is now the boss, he is now in charge. Even the tribe's chief dare not question the will of this god thing or its messenger.

Throw in many centuries and the whole church/god thing has grown into a

range of giant multi-national religions that have millions of followers.
(They have also branched out into other forms of money-making and/or control the masses enterprises such as schools, to get them while they're young and hospitals, to get them when they're sick and manuafacturing, to use cheap, god-fearing labour and make more money. But I digress.)

Decorated, embellished and made ornate and magnificent, their particular gods, ceremonies and rules may vary but they all use the same magic super word 'faith.'
It's a win/win for the religion because it is still based on human fear. When there's no physical evidence that any of these gods exist and you're running the risk of a credibility problem, you simply wheel out the magic word.
"Of course you must have faith." That's how it works. If you have faith that this unprovable, unfathomable fiction I am telling you is all true then this particular god (insert name here) will look out for and when you die .... You will be taken into some infinitely wonderful after-life where (insert anything you like here - free ice cream, dancing girls or men, beds with silk sheets) will be yours for eternity.
The death thing and a fabulous after-life is the clincher.
So the magic 'faith' word is used throughout the human world to control and manipulate people.
It is the 'power' the religions hold over their followers.

As an aside. What other human endeavour attracts people who like power?
Politics of course.
Note how closely religions and politics are blended throughout the world.
Not in modern western democracies you say. Separation of church and state you quote. Not so. Check the backgrounds of all your politicians. You may be sadly surprised how many have very strong religious beliefs and agendas.
It's why they're there.

Finally. If you are a religious person and you're reading this page. In other words, you have a 'faith'.

I do not suggest you -

1. Write to me and make threats because I dare to question your 'faith'.
2. Walk away from your 'faith'. (If it truly brings you comfort and happiness.)

What I do ask you to do (and this will be difficult) is to make a concerted effort to step outside your 'faith' for a moment and look at exactly what it is you are being asked to believe without question.

Approached from a neutral, intelligent perspective you may find that the whole thing is a house of cards and when examined closely it will collapse.

Belief in religions and gods and all the dogma that goes with them is dropping constantly throughout the world, as people become more informed and are able to make thoughtful, rational decisions.

Come join us, the sun still shines, birds sing and evolution continues to evolve.

Humans

What is it like not to be human?

What is it like not to be human? I don't know, I've always been 'human'. Herein lies a fundamental problem with being a human. We have no idea whether we're a particularly fine example of the evolution of a species or we're a throwaway failure? We're all there is in our domain. (Yes, there are those who would argue that there are millions of other species on planet earth and some show quite clever traits in their interaction with their surroundings but I think I'm on fairly safe ground when I say that we have the apex position on intelligence in this patch. And yes, we could sure be a lot smarter with some of the things we do ..... but .....)

Are our thoughts and ideas, our inventions and progress spectacular or mediocre?

As mentioned in The Universe we have this other problem of only ever being aware of being on planet earth. We've never chatted with the good folk on the third planet from Alpha Centauri (only 4.3 light-years away) or found that the species on Geliese 581c hadn't noticed us because our civilization appeared to them like some minor bacterial growth.

So for the moment, we'll have to muddle along on the assumption that we're doing okay.

Are we a pretty good example of the creation of life and it's evolutionary progress? Well no.

It's pretty obvious that we're a violent, easily distracted, rather pompous mixture of fine qualities and near madness. There's a long way to go on the evolutionary path before we could be considered an example of beauty and wisdom.

Though we probably score a few points for working that out ourselves.

If we do not destroy ourselves, in the fullness of time, evolution may clean out all our faults and we'll emerge as a credible species. Trouble is, by our standards and our current lifespan, evolution is a very slow process. Do we have the time to get ourselves right? How many other species may have started off in the universe only to self destruct before they worked out that their behaviour had

a terminal aspect or they destroyed their planet through neglect before they could work out how to find some other places to live? Sound familiar?
Can we make a go of it or are we destined to head down a dinosaur path of our own making?
I'd say it's 50/50.

To give ourselves some chance we'd need to get off earth and get to some other habitable planets, set up viable alternate civilizations and make them work. The massive distances, the time involved and the risk of failure suggest that this will not happen anytime soon.
What would be handy is if we could find a way to defeat or control gravity and fathom out a means of travelling at or beyond the speed of light and surviving. The answer may be that we can't leave or at least travel very far. (So colonising Mars might be about it.) The alternative could be to send our spores or some genetic capsule (a sort of reverse Prometheus action) in the hope that new life, new humans may spring or come into existence, adapt and grow on distant worlds. Some say it's how we got here a long time ago.
Then there's evolution. The average human in the 15th century was a much shorter, weak, unhealthy, malnourished, toothless individual who considered themselves very fortunate if they lived past 35 years. Of course, you and your mother had to survive birth and early childhood first and that was very problematic.

Now in the 21st century we're on average taller, straighter, healthier, smarter and have teeth.
Lifespans are in the eighties and it is common for many people to reach 100. Though this is a lot of progress in a very short time it is not necessarily evolution at work. It is more the work of better food, better living conditions, cleanliness, medicine and less ways to die. (Which is a type of evolution.)
By 2200, who knows, we may be over two metres tall, have larger brains and live past 150.

We may not die at all.

If the current research and experimentation with the human genome continues we will probably have moved way beyond these predictions and have specialised humans (Let's call them SPLIFS for specialised life-forms) made to order. Of course that will create a whole new complication between the people who feel that SPLIFS deserve recognition and rights and those who feel that SPLIFS are created and thus there for no other purpose than to serve and be used as planned.

From cheap workers to sex objects and more.

Female pregnancy may not be necessary. Private operators could be creating human-like creatures for specific tasks or this may not be the case because AI (artificial intelligence) has produced machines that can do the tasks more efficiently. In the critical balance of good and evil that seems to play out constantly in the human narrative, becoming involved in the design of life itself could go either way.

There is the real possibility that once gene manipulation becomes commonplace, the human race may split into a number of species. As with all such events there will inevitably be some that are by design or default, superior to others. Oh dear.

Dogs

There's so many lessons we learn ....

There's so many life lessons we learn from canis familiaris without knowing the lesson is taking place. Friendship, trust, loyalty, understanding, scratching, excitement, indifference, acceptance, just being ......   Sometimes it's just the simple act of existing. On a bright still, sunny day check a dog's expression if it is stretched out and at ease in the yard. Now that is bliss in dog form.
"Hey," you say, "wait a minute. I know a dog who is a mean, miserable bundle of seething hatred and malice. Its sole motivation in life is to make life hell for those around it and rip bits off you if you venture too close. Where's the serene, bringer of peace in that one."
Okay, you have me on a technicality. Some dogs, like humans, are just not in tune with being nice. Maybe it's their upbringing. If you have a rotten start in life and get all your life lessons from a person who is not at all a good role model and who treats you very badly then you have a right to develop a large 'chip on the shoulder.' Some dog breeds, it must be said, have a predisposition to being less than amiable.
I still maintain that if we did a statistical analysis of the situation, there'd be a massive skew in favour of 'nice' dogs relative to nice humans.

It comes from dog history. Generally thought to have all originated from wolves or similar. These creatures over time (lots of time) became part of human tribes and I dare say the humans found various uses or tasks for these half-wild creatures because times were tough and having some ex-wolf, mooching free room and board from the tribe would not be acceptable.
They may have been lost or abandoned pups taken in, raised and taught to assist a hunt, find certain foods or act as guards. Perhaps some attached themselves to human groups in order to obtain food scraps and in time a bond developed.
Only later when humans had progressed to settled areas that involved, structures, primitive farming and larger orderly habitats would the dogs slip into a new role, that of companionship. Even then they were expected to earn their keep so at about the same time there would also have been a bit of exper-

imenting with dog variants to produce progeny with specific, desirable traits. Overall it would still be a case of fulfilling a need (larger dog for hunting, small dogs for rabbits or sniffing out different plants for food) but if all went well, the added bonus of an agreeable nature. A pooch you could talk to while alone in the forest. Tell it your troubles and gain comfort from the 'all-knowing' look in their eyes. Once the concept caught on dogs had real future.

So we arrive at today's doggy kingdom, with so many types and breeds. There are the very popular 'you can't go wrong with this one' breeds, the 'will take a bit of work' breeds, the 'seriously, you bought a what? breeds and then there's the 'breeding gone nuts' breeds where the ability to produce a grotesque malformation of face and body was considered pleasing by some character with a lot of time on their hands and scant consideration of the quality of life of the result of their efforts.

Do dogs understand human emotions and needs? There have been studies that suggest they can at least detect moods and react accordingly. Other work suggests they can detect illness and disease in humans. Their nose is incredibly powerful. Could be they simply be responding to an olfactory signal? Whatever their clever doggy intuitions and methods they know a lot about interaction and saying the right thing at the right time. To those who are now hesitating with, "Wait a minute. Dogs can't speak. There's no 'saying the right thing.' I suggest to you that you, have not had the pleasure of knowing a dog with these abilities.

So, all humans should consider the benefits of having a dog available for close specialised assistance in the tribulations that life may present and also for the smaller issues and even the good times.
Dogs can handle it all with aplomb.
If you find yourself chatting to your hairy mate and suddenly feel a little foolish, stop and take a look at your dog's face. He will have that "it's okay my friend,

please continue" look on his face.
It's what dogs do.

(Note: In a similar situation a cat will be signalling - "Go away. You're tiresome. I don't need anything at the moment.)

Wine

..... a pleasing alcoholic beverage.

What clever human first discovered that the juice of grapes could be manipulated in such a way so as to make a pleasing alcoholic beverage? I doubt it compared to the finest products of the top wineries of the world today but everything has to start somewhere. (See other chapters questioning beginnings and ends.)
It is said that the nobility of Europe possibly lived their whole lives drinking nothing but wine.
Considering the quality of water in the middle ages it may have been a wise move though it would have eventually been their undoing. We cannot live on bread (or wine) alone, to quote somebody who once said that.
Wine fills that gap between strong liquor like whisky, bourbon, rum, brandy, gin and the voluminous other drink, beer. It is neither too little nor too much.
It is just right.
It has the other characteristic of being subtle. Even your favourite wines can vary greatly from year to year, swinging from average to magnificent depending on the weather, the whims of the world and the winemaker.
There are sufficient varieties in wine to satisfy the most fussy drinker and the most discerning taste. Bold reds for the person who likes a drink that has strength, delicate whites for those who seek a lighter palate. And everything in between.

At this point I must issue a note of caution. Wine is a temptress. If you enjoy wine for what it is, how it tastes and how enjoyable it is to drink then you are safe but if you become a slave to wine then you will morph into a very tedious and annoying person.
I refer of course to the expert, the connoisseur, the person who sees wine as an extension to their ego. They will describe a glass of a particularly enjoyable merlot as "lively on the palate with an undertone of blueberries, chocolate and lemon essence displaying a fine aromatic bouquet reminiscent of the heady vanilla cream finish of the 1948 late bottling of ……." Well you get the idea.
Wine is the juice of a grape taken to delightful levels of cleverness for our enjoy-

ment. If it ceases to be an enjoyable drink and becomes an accessory to theatrical ramblings or just something to be seen holding for a group photo then the whole point of its existence is lost.

The old countries of Europe spent a lot of time developing and perfecting their regional specialities and a lot more time protecting their assets from those who would steal their ideas and techniques and create rivals to their little niche in the world of wine.
Their efforts to protect their brand or type were largely successful and thus the rest of the world went off and did their own thing. It resulted in a much more diverse and intriguing range of wine varietals and the world is richer for it.
Today if you want a Burgundy, it must come from Burgundy but if you want similar but different (and possibly better) wine it may be a bottle of red from a place in the new world. Brilliant wines are no longer the exclusive domain of European countries. We're all enjoying more better and more best.
A certain old-world superiority complex in winemaking gave way to interest and then acceptance of the much wider world of exceptional wine production.
Good for egos and quality standards.

But enough of the potted history. The really good thing about wine is that it is so .... drinkable. Furthermore, it is the perfect accompaniment to food and good conversation.
There are those who maintain that the more wine that is consumed, the more interesting and robust the conversation becomes. Of course, this may just be the wine talking.
It probably is but if you're part of said group who are whiling away an afternoon with just wine, cheese and other tasty comestibles while you mine a rich vein of thoughts and ideas, you may by 5pm have invented an improved wheel or sorted out the very reason for our existence.
It is my experience that these amazing discoveries tend to pale upon examination the next day as various flaws hitherto unnoticed, present themselves when

seen in a stronger light.

Occasionally though, one little gem will get through the filtering process and remain unscathed. It is these plus the many, many others that didn't make it, that make wine a very worthwhile product for the betterment of humankind.

Health News. A number of studies have suggested that red wine consumed daily in moderation can have beneficial effects on your heart and other organs. While certianly not empirical in their conclusions I felt it only fair to assist these medical folk by conducting a similar study. I can report, so far, so good.

NB Finally, keep in mind the oft repeated Latin phrase 'in vino veritas' (in wine, there is truth) and don't divulge too many secrets while imbibing, that you may later regret.

Emotions

Can you explain madness to a mad person ....

We all have them. Excitement, boredom, love, disgust, respect and on and on. They're the ups and downs of our interaction with other humans and the way we feel about ourselves every day.

Draw a line on a piece of paper. Put a little vertical line at each end. This line represents your emotional state. It may bump up and down along this line as your life progresses and different forces affect your emotional state but generally, we stay somewhere on this line.

For some of us, our emotional state becomes extreme. It could be some major to catastrophic event or it may be nothing more than our mind wandering off course and losing its ability to find a way back. This is where you have moved past those little stoppers at the end of your line and have entered a reality that is incomprehensible.

I once asked a psychiatrist, "How can you explain madness to a mad person." He replied, "You can't. Like any person, we have our sets of values and our sense of what is real. You can only work as a guide and rearrange the furniture so that they find their own way back. Many don't know they ever left and so have no sense of having returned."

Rather poetic but it did sum up the vagaries of emotions.

Which brings us to the many new, contrived forces being placed upon our emotions.

The people for instance, working in marketing spend a great deal of time researching us, collecting and analysing data about us and applying all sorts of emotional hooks to enthuse us about their products.

Then there's politics, sporting allegiances, religions, charities, entertainment, movies and television. So many interests tugging at us in a bid to secure an emotional response. A sea through which to navigate.

At times, of course, we suppress emotions in order not to offend or to fit into a social group or situation. Who has not been in a gathering where conversations and opinions are opposed to your own opinions? Yet you remain silent or compliant because it would not be in the interest of all parties to express an alternate point of view. To keep the peace as it were.

Some would argue that 'robust' exchange of views is always preferable but it is how wars begin and there is a rather warm smugness in walking away knowing your opinion is more valid. And the other silent witnesses probably felt the same.

I know somebody whose advertising business had a slogan which read: 'Advertising - the reason you know you need something you didn't know you needed.'

Although it applies to advertising this phrase equally summarises all the bombardment our emotions receive on a daily basis. It is hard in an age of almost 'too much information' to absorb, sort and evaluate responses to the vast array of attacks our psyche takes while we go about our lives. By attack, I mean news, television, radio, billboards, posters, internet, phone, even putting fuel in your car now has screens on the pumps belting out a message.

So we adopt a defensive position and switch off. Through all the burble and roar in the background, we just focus. This solves the problem but turns us into uncaring automatons who may often miss genuinely nice moments or a chance to be kind or helpful.

An elderly neighbour of mine related a story to me of going to buy some goods downtown. He noticed the small store carpark was full as he drove in the entrance. Then a man and his son emerged and climbed into their car. A spot was about to become available. The man then pulled out and did about a 6 point turn so that he finished up facing my neighbour waiting to pull in. Instead of just moving back to let my neighbour into the parking spot or backing away and going out the exit he insisted that he wanted to head out the entrance. Words were exchanged. In the end my neighbour backed off and let the man out. As the man went past, despite being in the wrong, he delivered his killer blow. "Stupid old man," he yelled. "That's the bit that hurt," said my neighbour.

"No apology, no thank you. Just an assumption that I'm old, so I don't matter and I'm stupid. No wonder humans have wars."

I apologised to him on behalf of the slightly younger generation.

He had a point. Humans have a history of letting their emotions override sense. It is an overdeveloped ego, a pride, a sense of entitlement that has done us no good at all throughout history.

Emotions are part of the package you get when you come into existance. Like a dog on a leash who gets off to run in the park, we can sometimes, in a suitable area, let our emotions off the leash. However, if the dog starts heading for the edge of the park and that busy road, it's time to call it back. Same with emotions.

Ideas

How many great ideas obtain life?

Somewhere there should be a giant organisation, free of all bias and prejudice, which can assess every idea as it is born, give it due consideration and allow it to live or die depending on its worth. What a marvellous world we would have if such a place existed.

How many great ideas obtain life? Not many. Meanwhile, how many bad ideas seem to find credence and get a run when they should not? Quite a lot.

If ideas are considered as creative thought then there's hardly a branch of human endeavour where it cannot be argued that the overwhelming output is mediocre to terrible. Have you heard people say, "Surely there's a better way to do this" or "I can't believe we haven't thought of a way around this problem." Sadly there probably is and somebody probably has but opportunity, timing, greed, self preservation, brand protection, control, power, connections, jealousy and so on have all combined to bury the great idea, the brilliant answer while powerful forces pump out more of the bad stuff.

Inventors, writers, artists, musicians, philosophers, medical researchers, engineers, scientists, etc have without doubt over the centuries had their work dismissed or stay unheard and unseen because, let's call it 'fate', has worked against them.

Others have died before their genius was noticed or had their work stolen and never received recognition. There are also many cases of the creators of great ideas that have changed the world dying in poverty years later.

The really terrifying thought is the possibility that some truly massive ideas that could hvae changed and improved the world have never seen the light of day. At this moment we may be searching for the answer to a great puzzle in science or medicine without knowing that the answer was discovered some time ago and allowed to disappear.

That's the negative side of the ideas game. Now let's examine the positive. Lot's of ideas do make it through the race to the finish line and the world in which we live is the way it is because of these people.

One unsung hero from the past is the person who took a look at a fire, perhaps caused by a lightning strike and thought, "there must be a way to keep this fire thing going and even carrying it around." Then somebody else figured out ways to actually start a fire. Followed by the person who first stuck a bit of meat in the fire and discovered cooking. History does not record their achievements but we are all grateful for their work. Not to mention the man or woman who first thought of sticking a couple of wheels on the tribe's sled. Possibly followed soon after by the brake mechanism.

Now, of course, there's money, lots of it, to be made from great ideas, from better toilet paper to space flight. So idea factories exist in many industries to advance ways and means of doing things and accomplishing goals.

Strangely, it is often the person working alone who has the really great breakthrough.

Without the restraints of a corporate structure guiding their thoughts, they are able to see more clearly and think outside the square.

If anybody out there has come up with an anti-gravity device and a faster than light transporter please give me a call. You may have something worthwhile.

If you have an idea, give it a chance, let it run free. It may fail and fall but it may also grow and become magnificent and make you proud.

You can use the opposite page to make a note of your idea/s. If there's not enough room you'll find extra pages at the back of this book.

Art and Expression

..... remarkable and beautiful things.

Despite our numerous faults we humans do have a creative side that, over time, has produced some remarkable and beautiful things.
Not all are rewarded. I remember once visiting a giant Alhambra in Spain and standing away from the other tourists for a moment, trying to take in the sheer magnificence of the intricate fretwork that made up part of the building.
The artisan who created this amazing work was just some worker who was never recognised and is lost to history. Yet the work is as equal in importance as many of the great and well-known architects and their achievements.
Art was confined for much of human history to depicting only images of our various Gods. The ongoing power and control obsession that religions have regarding the population.

Come the Renaissance and artists began to question this limited range of subjects. Some had been sneaking little bits of landscape and decoration into the background of their works for years but now there was full-on rebellion as painters completed whole works that showed no Gods at all, just a
pleasing scene of some misty mountains or a placid lake. It didn't take long for the wealthy and their bloated egos to get involved and portraits of fat, satisfied, highly decorated upper-class folk became the norm.
(Most portraits from the past are probably not faithful renditions of the subject. Any artist wanting to stay in favour and get paid would include a certain artistic licence whilst commtting the purchaser to canvas. The secret was a subtle improving of the sitter's appearance whilst avoiding the too obvious.)

While western art led the way, there is and was quite incredible beauty in the traditional art and expression of many countries.

This section is called 'Art and Expression' and it is a bit like trying to describe how to build a particle accelerator in a few sentences. Let's leave art (ie visual) for a moment and consider that practically any human endeavour done well or exceptionally well or beautifully is art or expression. A poet is expressing feelings and ideas, so is an author but who is to say that a carpenter putting heart and soul into a pannelled room is not 'creating' something wonderful.

The notion that art can be found anywhere is often explored by installation art. Boundaries are pushed and many of us find it hard to be delighted by say a large room at the gallery in which there is a lone toilet seat with a can of chicken soup on top.Viewers get angry, laugh, dismiss, feel cheated, walk out but mostly cry, "This is not art."
To a large degree, they're right. Until you ask the question, "What is art?" Then you're into the whole crazy, often naive world that you inhabit when you're young. The world where you question, discuss, dismiss everything and every notion because you're convinced you know everything and there is a better way.
It's the very silliness and bravery of art that produces so much terrible stuff and occasionally a real gem. A painting, a sculpture, a photograph, a book, a play, a movie, whatever it is, there is a moment when most agree this one is a real keeper. A genuine, bonafide masterpiece.

Of course, we are fickle beings and the masterpiece status may be fleeting. We change, we question, discuss, dismiss previous norms and the whole process evolves. The words of an author once quoted in hushed tones, now become trite and 'out-of-touch'. We decide we know better and a new direction for enlightened thinking is created.
Is it better?
Are we being pretentious?
It's a human thing. We are driven on by leaving the past behind. Call it progress or simply change.

So, art is whatever we currently define as art with numerous terms, conditions and caveats.

Expression is a more pure beast. It contains passion, tears, hope and blindness all in a wonderful mix.
(I've always felt that philosophers were frustrated artists not brave enough to give way to their inner urges.)

Humans like to create but it tends to be a luxury. Starving people, those in danger or despair do not afford themselves the indulgence of pausing in the daily fight for existence to put down some deep thoughts or bring into being profound images.

If the urge takes hold of you then it may be that you should give in and let the forces take control.
Paul Gauguin gave up a comfortable life in Paris and headed for Tahiti.
There he led a fairly austere life and spent a lot of time with the local Tahitians who feature in most of his paintings. He seems to have been happy and he left us some of the world's most renowned paintings.
(There would have been more but accounts suggest some of his work may have been thrown in the sea by a creditor and some burned as pornography. Art has this habit of upsetting the public.)

You may not have to move to Tahiti but it's worth consideration.

Landscape

I've no idea what it looks like elsewhere ......

I've no idea what it looks like elsewhere. None of us do. We've all only lived on earth. We can only make educated guesses as to what it might be like to stand on one of two newly discovered earth-like planets orbiting Teegarden's star a mere 12.5 light-years away.

Earth-like is a very broad definition of a planet's attributes. Certain references such as colour spectrums can give tiny clues to the possibility of breathable air and liquid water but that's a long way from a verdant paradise that would suit us as an earth substitute or twin. Then there's the currently insurmountable task of actually transporting some live humans to this new earth.

(It occurs to me that if a planet has a whole list of earth-like properties, the same properties that allow us to live and breathe and reproduce, then there is every chance that it already supports life. A life form that may be hostile, primitive or highly advanced. Whatever the case the life form would probably not be excited about an armada of spacecraft arriving overnight, full of creatures who have plans to settle on their planet.)

So, our earth, earth 1, this planet on which we live, it's our home and if the weather is good and all is well then we're presented, in different parts of our world with pleasing vistas that make us happy, content and love our planet. We take pictures, paint paintings and admire the beautiful aspect of the scenery before us.

Of course, if our eyes had evolved differently and we were receptive to another part of the electro-magnetic spectrum then the blue sky, green trees and other wonders of nature would appear in an entirely other colour range. Infra-red perhaps.

But enough of the science, let's get down to the intestines of the beast. Attachment to and longing for a particular part the planet with which you are familiar is as much a part of the human condition as breathing itself. We are part of the landscape as much as it is part of us. Australian aboriginal people take this connection to the land to a whole higher plane of existence whereby their very being (soul if you like) is part of the landscape. They do not see the earth as something to be owned but more a bond between their body and the earth on which it dwells.

We all know our feeling of disconnection when we travel and are away from surroundings that are familiar and comforting. Places where we grew and made our pact with the ground upon which we walked. It may be somewhere like a beautiful forest and a lake, an oceanside with roaring waves or a harsh, angry, dry place with broken rock and mountains or desert. To those who know and have memories of it then it is the place that they belong and are drawn to when they need peace.

I have travelled and seen many different parts of this planet. Some have been beautiful, some not so much but in all of them there were people who knew and loved their particular niche. To outsiders, their attachment may seem puzzling. You wish you could explain to them that their special place is not as good as some others you could name. Of course, you forget that it is to do with belonging. Having some soil that you can pick up and let run through your fingers and say this is my part of the earth, on which I dwell. It is in me, it is part of me. For me personally, there is a piece of landscape with a mixture of sights, sounds and smells (particularly after rain) that will always bring great contentment.
I doubt I could explain it to another but I know it.

If humans can ever find the technology to reach another liveable planet they may, in generations, become attached to whatever landscape they find on their new home. It's part of a sense of belonging.
Whether us earthlings would agree will depend on the images they send back showing the new house, the garden and that dog-like creature they call Fido.

Landscape is memory. Like a child to a parent once the imprint is made on our psyche it will be with us until our death.

And in most cases, we are then returned to the landscape, become part of and add to another generation's landscape.

Earth

It's our home address ....

It's our home address. The place where we live. It is incredibly fragile. Everything about earth that makes it a reasonably good place to live is, in the grand scheme of the universe, momentary and subject to change.

The earth it seems will not last forever. If you are saddened by the thought of the Grand Canyon or the tranquil Pacific Ocean being lost, I suggest that all such things will have long since morphed into some other geological form many times over before the earth is no more.

We humans may have died out many millions of years before or more optimistically we may have moved on to some even better planets and abandoned dear old earth as a rather second-rate place to live.

Our earth has a nice breathable atmosphere consisting mainly of nitrogen and oxygen but there's not a lot of it. Most of it is in the first 16kms above the surface. If we travel just 3kms from the surface into the troposphere we can't really breath. About 20kms above the surface is the start of the stratosphere. This is where we find the ozone layer which doubles as a radiation shield and a blanket to retain heat.

Above the stratosphere at about 50kms up is the mesosphere which is very cold and handily causes meteors to burn up. And so it goes.

Our earth is a critical balance of all the necessities we require for life.

From polar ice caps to liquid water to plant life to filtered sunlight to temperature to landmass ....

A myriad of life forms, of creatures, have come into being and have existed or still exist yet they could all cease to exist if just one part of our life support balance became unbalanced.

Despite the precarious nature of our existence, we treat this lifeboat to which we cling, as it makes its way through space, with a degree of contempt bordering on arrogance.

It's as if the earth was just some temporary place we are staying at for a few days before moving on to a better, more secure world.

If readers have noticed a slight theme in this book it is that I feel the human race has ideas and expectations of its own importance and invincibility far outweighing reality.

The planet earth does not owe us a living. It does not care if we survive or not. Earth just exists and in this particular time and place and its conditions are such that we are able to exist on it and evolve. As our only place to live at present and with little chance of finding and reaching another earth-like habitat for the foreseeable future we really need to do a little housekeeping.

Dispense with wars, conquests, religions, kings, greed and despots and look after this place before we become just another failure in the universal soup that sometimes brings forth life.

When we lived in caves and the only danger we represented was to the occasional passing, edible beast we were of little consequence to the planet's survival. Now however we have become clever and our reach across the landforms of earth is global. Now our machines, our wants, our needs have become dangerously over-ambitious. We are becoming a global threat.

If we annoy the planet enough it may decide to retaliate. A thousand years of unsustainable heat or another prolonged ice-age should see us gone and planet earth can then resume its gentle comfortable existence for lots more millions of years.

At the moment it's heat that is the issue. The global temperature is rising.

The earth has had heating and cooling events before in its long history. But such happenings took hundreds or thousands of years to evolve. Not the rapid escalation we see today.

There does seem to be a stirring amongst the populations of the earth that all is not good. Finally the message that climate scientists have been shouting out for some time are being heard. Whether those who care can put a stop to those don't is the tipping point.

So .....

If we have found ways to destroy ourselves on such a global scale and thus we are gone or clinging to hope on a ruined planet, just waiting for the last flickerings of life to switch to darkness.

Then the game is ours to win or lose.

The planet, in time, will rebuild and continue. In a few million years, no trace of our existence will remain.

It's our call. There's no plan B.

Trees

They're just the right size ....

They're just the right size for us humans, to provide comfort, shelter, grand vistas, wood and a breathable atmosphere through photosynthesis. No wonder we like trees.
Overall there's not many negatives about trees. Personally, I like being alone with a big tree. No, I have never heard one speak but I'm sure they're listening I have childhood memories of a large Jacaranda tree that grew in our yard. Its soft fronds and purple flowers would cover the grass in summer and stick to my bare feet. Our dog loved its cool shady understorey.

Trees were once unique to different parts of the earth. If you were in Northern Europe you would see a lot of their particular larch, spruce or Siberian pine.
In more southern parts of Europe were beech, ash, poplar and willows.
In North America maples, dogwood and sycamore. In South America mahogany, rosewood, coral trees and monkey puzzle pines. In Asia magnolia, almond, cypress, mulberry, walnut, buckthorn.
In Australia the completely unique range of eucalypts or gum trees, silky oaks and the living fossil the Wollemi pine.
Of course, being human and never being happy with what's in our own backyard we started moving things about all over the earth until now, depending on climate and suitability, no tree is entirely unique to any area, although most major forests tend to still be genuine locals.
(Forests are grand and many are vast. But like the ocean, they can be treacherous. Play on the edges, make journeys across but don't get lost or you may not be seen again. Fairy tale stuff - also reality.)

Trees are great to have around. Since humans first evolved to stand upright, create tools, build shelters and plant crops we've had an overwhelming desire to cut down every tree we encountered.
If the big tree's roots are undermining your house then it has to go but removing vast forests for very dubious reasons involving greed are very short-sighted. Much of the world we first evolved into was covered in forests. In fact we hu-

mans probably wouldn't be here if it wasn't for trees whose high branches initially gave us safety from predators.

Then we advanced rapidly and needed more land to plant our food, we needed timber to build our houses, furniture, early tools and carts. We needed lots of wood to burn for heat and cooking. Trees were an endless commodity. Besides if you cut them down others would grow in their place. Win, win.

Until we reached a critical point in the tree plan where demand raced ahead of supply. The factories of Europe belched out smoke from burning coal and wood. Forests disappeared to make room for more factories. The air became toxic and unbreathable. Less trees meant less good air. More factories meant more bad air.
Keep in mind that trees are not trying to do us air-breathers a favour. In fact the oxygen they put out is really a byproduct of their little water plus carbon dioxide process. We should be very grateful that it works out the way it does.

Have we learnt a lesson and put a stop to this destruction? Well, only a bit. Yes, nice suburbs in nice cities have tree policies and can be leafy and green but meanwhile the 'world's lungs', the Amazon rainforest continues to disappear at an alarming rate and large swathes of Asian jungle are being razed in order to produce palm oil.
Like so many human activities it is hoped we will learn our lesson and stop.

There are still good news stories. The Wollemi National Park near Sydney Australia is so large, rugged and unexplored that it was only a few years ago that a species of an amazing ancient pine tree was discovered that dated back to dinosaur days. Only fossils had ever been seen. Deep in a steep, heavily forested canyon, living specimens were found. The Australians did something very smart. Instead of guarding the tree and hoping it would survive they took lots of seeds and started growing Wollemi pines in greenhouses. Once stocks are sufficiently built up they will be for sale and thus no longer rare and endangered. Presumably, in a few years somebody in New York, London or Paris could have one in their front garden. (Warning - They're rather large.)

Should we hug trees? It was very fashionable a while back. I say, why the hell not. Such habits should not die out. As you press your face against your chosen tree's sturdy frame and feel its bark against your cheek say, "Hullo my friend, it is really good to know you."
Should you be observed, turn to the observer and invite them to join you. Tree's can have more than one friend.

People

It's so easy. People are like sheep ....

A person I have known all my life works in marketing.
He tells me 'people are sheep.'
He is constantly amazed at how easily people can be manipulated and controlled. It makes his job so very easy. While he uses his powers for good, in that he figures out ways to sell people certain products and services, it is not a particularly large leap to see these same marketing techniques being employed in all sorts of nefarious activities.
Although not strictly criminal, politics and religion immediately spring to mind. We find people being manipulated into carrying out crimes against their fellow humans, based on ideologies that when viewed from afar, by a clear unbiased mind, prove to be without any merit and simply the work of malicious, dictatorial power people.

Sit on a train or bus and observe your current contemporaries. What are they all doing? They're staring at their phones. They're so completely attached to these small electronic devices that psychologists have coined the phrase 'nomophobia' to cover the obsession. Take away and deprive many people the use of their mobile phone and you have a psychotic episode in the making.
In an ever more crowded world, average humans are becoming herd-like in their behaviour. We must be attached to the world by this electronic umbilical cord or we wither and die.

School bullying has taken on a whole new dimension with the added weapons of social media. The person being harrassed can simply turn off the sources of the attack and tell those involved they are wasting their time because he/she won't be watching. But they can't. It is now in their DNA to stay connected.

Fame. It was once a position you attained in society by your deeds or exploits, good or bad. Fame is now a commodity. Communication has made it so. With all the world connected, people need instant and ongoing gratification and this is provided by famous people. Though for many the fame is brief because we need a constant supply of shiny new famous people.

The deeds and exploits of these persons is almost irrelevant. It is simply enough that they are famous for people to worship them.

To be near to somebody famous has a drug-like effect. As if their aura may provide onlookers with some input of energy.

Royal families like the British, whose only contribution to society is to be born, have turned their current flock of young royals into an ongoing pageant of fame. People adore them for doing nothing except being royal. They still command and are head of state over large parts of their old empire. They serve no useful purpose and in practical terms should have been conveyed to the dustbin of history a long time ago, yet they stay.

This brings us to the sad truth about being a person. You conform to a thing called 'lifestyle.' Even non-conformists are caught in its tentacles. Lifestyle is a fluid thing. Accepted norms of today will be ridiculed, even laughed at a few years down the track. Part of this is continued advancement in learning, invention, medicine and technology but unfortunately, a lot of it is just the rambling silliness of the age. There are 'lifestyle' gurus now. Slick people who have invented a totally confected persona that apparently gives them the right to dictate how others should think, feel, dress themselves and behave.

We obey and continue to listen to their message.

It is not a new thing but it is a human thing. Every age has had its absurdities of fashion and odd to crazy ideas about how to act and what is good or bad. Perhaps now we have entered an age of shallowness. With 'devices' such as mobile phones, mobile computers and pads we are connected to a strange other-world at all times. (Unless your battery is flat or you're out of range in which case you either go into advanced panic mode or briefly enjoy a different and possibly fulfilling life until reconnected.)

We like to pretend that this new connectivity means we are all now one giant, generally happy world. Of course, we are not. We're isolated, unaware of our

surroundings and judge our daily success or failure by how many pointless, unnecessary communications we make with others in the other-world. All the time the real world is right there around us but we no longer notice it.
Is being able to look up answers and knowledge almost instantly a step forward or backward? Are we losing our ability to seek out answers and knowledge by having it so freely available online?

We play games where the purpose is killing, death and mayhem yet nobody dies and you can instantly revive and reboot. The new generations seem to have become these odd, half-grown child-people who do not want to leave their young self behind in adulthood. Entertainment such as movies is now geared to producing comic book style features to cash in on these adults who have not crossed over.

The disenfranchised of our society, the disturbed, angry, unhappy, frustrated were once isolated by their view of the world and lived out their lives in a cocoon of bitterness, unable to voice their annoyance at their fellow humans. Now they can sit in their rooms and easily find other like-minded souls who want to discuss their frustrations. Free and oddly anonymous they pass each other angry messages that seek revenge for all the wrongs they perceive. There is a whole network now of people whose troubled view of the world often breaks out in acts of aggression and murder as they organise each other to make a statement for whatever particular cause they feel justifies their actions.
Is there a point where this other-world and the real world start to blur and merge. Where we can no longer tell one from the other?

Which comes back to the original hypothesis. People are sheep. They can be herded, manipulated, shorn and slaughtered and in most cases, they'll let it happen and not even be aware that it is happening,

Rituals

We humans love rituals ....

We, humans, love rituals. From the moment we had a rational thought I'd imagine we put our next mental energies into decorating the thought with pomp and ceremony. Armed forces, sport, politics, even why and how you do things around the office all require odd little bits of superfluous, frippery that allows us to take part in some 'ritual.'

Of course the grandmasters of multi-layered ornamentation, to the point of absurdity, are the two Rs. Religion and Royalty.

My marketing friend has a quite reasonable explanation for such behaviour. (And he may be right.)

If you have nothing to sell, if what you are offering adds up to a great big box of zero, then you hide it with lots of decorations and ritual.

His example is two packets of very ordinary laundry powder. They are in fact identical from the same manufacturer. One is in a plain box marked laundry powder. The other is in a highly decorated shiny box with pictures of frangipanis and pine forests. It is called
'Magipowa Supa Mist'.

There are words like 'Supawash', 'Superior Clean', 'Sparkling Fresh.'

Magipowa is twice the price of the plain pack but it must be good, just look at the packaging.

It is why a concept such as God evolves. A stationary God would be overtaken by common sense and enlightened thinking. So the concept is reinvented as required. The God of the middle ages bears no resemblance to the contemporary sales pitch that is used to sell modern God. There are switched on new churches with rock bands and lots of hand-clapping and use of credit cards or eft donations.

Modern royal families are sold more as pop star celebrities than the old all-powerful, off with his/her head characters of the past.

In both cases, the members of the inner circle of religions or royals realise their grip on power and influence is fading so they must find new ways to appear to be even vaguely relevant in current society. Rituals are very much part of this image reinvention.

The strength of the argument for obsessive ritual making can be seen across the world. Natives in a jungle, people scraping by in a desert existence, humans of all types whose life is a day to day struggle still have time for rituals. What they wear, what they say and do, think and feel are all bound up by some form of ritualistic behaviour.
For those from another culture, their particular rituals may seem strange and pointless through to utterly absurd. Yet observers who scorn would be wise to look within, for almost certainly they too are adherents to their own brand of rituals.
Next time you're at a funeral, a sports fixture, a party, a fishing trip, a symphony concert, any gathering of people, step back mentally and take note of how many little unnecessary odd behaviours and patterns take place. Rituals are so ingrained in our psyche that we do not notice them as anything other than normal behaviour or just the way things are done. Etiquette is just silly rituals by another name.

I must say though, religion does take No.1 spot in the rituals department because they have the most amount of nothing to sell. The clear second is royalty and royal families for similar reasons, then it's probably a tie for third between politics and armed forces.
Both of these 3rd placegetters like to distract participants from the real goings-on by creating a great deal of pomp and ceremony.
You may think that religion, royalty and military are way in front with their funny hats, highly decorated outfits and endless 'secret society' approach to their craft but politicians are just more subtle. Their little rituals are so that the public miss what they're actually doing and armed forces, of course, wish to draw your attention away from the fact that their occupation is inherently

dangerous with a major death aspect to it.

As you can see it is easy to mock rituals, until you do a little self-examination and realise that you too have collected a whole range of quirky but somehow necessary behaviour patterns in your life and your social interaction.
From the pseudo superstitious such as touching wood, black cats and ladders to the quite serious ceremonies at say a school graduation or sports finals when if examined objectively, mean very little but to participants, the whole process gives a feeling of accomplishment and completion which could not be achieved by a simple letter in the mail.

We do what we do because we are human and that's the way the world we live in operates. Hundreds of years ago the rituals may have been different and many years hence they may have whole new levels of wizardry and sophistication but they will still just be rituals.
It seems we need them.

Power

Everybody wants power ....

Everybody wants power. We may not admit it, even deny any such thoughts but it is there, buried deep in the psyche of every human. Not necessarily the power to smite those who displease you and make the oceans bend to your will, it may be as simple as having the power to climb out of abject poverty and find food and shelter for your family.

History is strewn with powerful people. However, most historians would be hard-pressed to name an all-powerful figure from the past who has left behind a legacy of joy, fulfillment and happiness.
We, humans, are just not very good with power. The moment we get some of it we seem to lose our sense of balance, fairness, right and wrong. It's simple 'power corrupts.'
Not many people have heard of John Dahlberg, 1st Baron of Acton but most would have heard quoted or misquoted his opinion that, "Power tends to corrupt and absolute power corrupts absolutely."
It sums up our problem quite succinctly.

One way round our lust for power was to head down the road to fantasy. If we could not have great power ourselves we simply invented other beings that did possess such attributes. And because we the unpowerful invented these powerful beings we gave them an inclination to do good things and to deny (often with extreme prejudice) those who did not. Comic book superheroes were born and judging from the current trends in entertainment from Hollywood we still like the cut of their jib.

Back in the real world we have numerous examples of good people gone bad and bad people who got worse. None who got better. The best we can do is there's a number who stayed okay.
Now some may argue that there are powerful people in the world who are essentially good.
Royalty for instance. They're powerful, aren't they? Generally, they're okay?

Well no. All the royals of the world today, the heirs of once powerful and generally horrible Kings and Queens of yesteryear are now just figureheads. They have a fair amount of wealth but they have no real power.
French philosopher Denis Diderot once said, "Man will never be free until the last king is strangled with the entrails of the last priest." He summed up the mood of the times beautifully. Not long after he wrote these words the 'French Revolution' took place. Today the French have no royalty though they do still have priests.
So his utterances regarding freedom have only half been fulfilled.

This brings me to another quote. Karl Marx said, "Religion is the Opium of the masses."
He was recognising the undeniable fact that religion and religious dogma is an incredibly powerful tool by which millions and millions of people throughout the world are manipulated, exploited and controlled by a few. The threat here comes not from the religious leaders making direct threats to their followers but instead using the subliminal messaging in their particular brand of teachings to subjugate people with the dreadful consequences if they should stray or disobey. It's a winner. The first and best 'Catch 22'.

It's why so often we see hybrid powerful people. Such is their love of power that they try the power of religion and after finding it to their liking decide for a double-dose by entering politics. Still more power.
Of course, if you ask most people how they think they would handle great power they will invariably state that they would be first-rate altruistic users of said power and bring great happiness and well-being to all without favour.

A Small Example
A musician friend of mine mentioned that the power thing is a big issue in bands. When he told me I could see what he meant. A group of musicians is a perfect microcosm of the power problem. It is ongoing and it seems the more

damage it will cause the more the chance of it happening.

Once one band member realises that their role is sufficiently important to cause a great deal of harm if they were to leave then the urge to do so and cause major disruption overcomes their values of decency, loyalty and fairness. Even if their walking out will also cause them to lose a great deal in wasted time and lost opportunity, the lust for wielding their power is just too tempting.

In opera circles, it's known as the 'prima donna factor.'

A Large Example

Karl Marx saw a world of infinite cooperation. It was a form of existence whereby the state was the people and the people were the state. Where everybody worked for the common good and their work was shared and all were equal. This ideal, utopian wish for a perfect human existence has a lot of appeal, especially if you happen to be part of that large worldwide demographic that is poor and downtrodden. It must seem like the answer to all your woes. It has one fatal flaw.

Many countries embraced communism, others had it forced upon them but in every place where communism has been allowed to blossom, it has quickly turned from a wonderful open and fair society into a quite harsh authoritarian dictatorship. That fatal flaw, of course, is human misuse of power and the inevitable slide into autocracy where power itself is a corrupting force.

Where does this leave us everyday folk with a hidden desire for a little power but getting on with our lives anyway? Fairly content as far as I can see. It's all to do with perspectives. You'd like to be powerful and sort out the world a little but reality says 'no'. So you do the next best thing. You watch those with power very, very carefully because you know that deep down they are going to be tempted to cross over to the dark side. This is your job, to stand on the border with all the other everyday folk hands outstretched. As the powerful ones approach the border you say in a very loud and powerful voice, "Go back. You don't belong here."

Bread and Chocolate

It is good and bad at once ....

It is good and bad at once. There are not too many human inventions that can provide such a soothing touch to our daily routine while adding a range of harmful ingredients to our gut.

Chocolate came in its basic form from the Aztecs. It was consumed as a drink and was probably much more bland, almost bitter, compared to the sweet concoction we know today.

You see, we humans, to our detriment have become obsessed with sugar. Once a fairly pricey commodity sugar is now a staple (along with salt) in just about everything we eat. So chocolate is now quite sweet. And comes in so many disguises it is hard to spot.

My favorite fruit brioche I noticed has recently replaced its raisins with chocolate chips.

Chocolate seems to be like a house guest who we know is evil, yet is so charming and likeable that we haven't the heart to turn them out and restore order. Still, few things in life are more rewarding than fine coffee or tea and some high-quality chocolate.

Suddenly your troubles seem less significant and are solvable. All it took was some of that delightful creamy, brown substance to melt gently on your tongue and slide past your tastebuds and down your throat. "Ahh, bliss."

Chocolate has various levels of quality and thus various levels of ingredients but let us look at a decent mid-range piece of European chocolate. (NB There is no point using any US manufactured chocolate because laws are so lax regarding the product's contents that it generally bears little resemblance to actual chocolate and is chocolate in name only. It's why European chocolate tastes so good. Because it is actually chocolate.)

First and foremost is the ingredient that makes chocolate really chocolate. Cacao beans grow mostly in Africa. The seeds of the cacao tree are very bitter so they must be fermented to produce the flavor. After fermentation, the beans are dried and cleaned then roasted. The shell is then removed and the resulting

cacao nibs are ground to cocoa mass. This is chocolate in its raw form.
The cocoa mass is liquefied by heating and becomes chocolate liquor.
This liquor is also cooled and processed into two components: cocoa solids and cocoa butter.
Overall chocolate contains sugar, cocoa butter, full cream milk powder, cocoa liquor, lecithin, vanilla and cocoa.

Not a lot of vitally healthy items in that list but put them all together and you just can't beat the unique and magical taste that is chocolate.
Give in.

Bread, on the other hand, is generally healthy. It comes in far too many forms throughout the human world to be listed here but overall it is made from the flour of a grain that is formed into a dough and baked or heated to form an edible product.
Most traditional bakers rise early while we're sleeping so that they can have bread ready for us during the day. This gives bread a nice romantic touch. Anybody who has visited a warm bread shop on a cold morning and stood breathing in the aromas of the ovens knows that there are few more fulfilling experiences. As chocolate is an indulgence, bread is a staple.
A part of life and living. Though too much can still be unhealthy.

Ancient archeological sites have revealed bread and bread making. There were loaves for sale in Pompei and Herculaneum when Vesuvius struck. Egyptian Pharaohs were partial to a bit of bread.
Perhaps it is bread's versatility that makes it so popular. From a crusty baguette with hot soup to a giant sandwich made with thick slices of wholemeal, to a pizza fresh from the oven to chapati or naan with your curry, the flour to dough mix is a winner.
In the early days of Australia, cattlemen and settlers produced a very simple

bread called damper. It could have as few ingredients as flour, salt and water. Generally it was cooked in a iron camp oven using coals from the fire.

The result is a beautiful golden, crunchy, round loaf. It was eaten with meat or beans.

I can verify that damper, covered in butter and honey or treacle, together with a cup of hot tea or coffee while resting by a campfire, can make life very satisfying.

No doubt similar stories can be told of the pioneers of America and Canada. Wherever there's a lot of land to be explored.

So, chocolate or bread? If you find that you have an urge to indulge in either of these products I can only repeat, give in, treat yourself. If you then feel a certain amount of guilt that is also fine, in fact, it's part of the experience.

To 'ere is human, after all.

Here's a back-handed health tip. If you indulge repeatedly every day then the experience will be less enjoyable. Limit yourself, thus making the final collapse of willpower a little more exotic.

Life

a period of expansion followed by contraction ....

In its basic form, all life seems to follow a pattern of expansion followed by contraction. No, not life followed by death. That's too simplistic. While life still exists there is a turning point, an apex beyond which the life goes no further and begins to retreat. With perhaps a few stutterings of resistance, this contraction continues throughout the second phase of the lifeform until there life no more.

A sad inevitable conclusion.

Life is in fact a terrible disease that ultimately results in death.

There is no cure …. yet.

How did life happen anyway? What the hell is life? Well, it's the coming together of various elements. The current school of thought is that there needs to be 25 of the basic elements for life to begin. Of those, the really important ones are sulfur, phosphorous, oxygen, nitrogen, carbon, and hydrogen. In that order they make a mnemonic to help you remember. It all really hinges on carbon and its versatility. And carbon can go in many directions so we should not assume that our form of life is unique.

Let's not go any further into the vastly complex set of circumstances and chances involved in the coming together of all the componentry that eventually produced something that was not just a chemical reaction but gained that added spark and became a 'living' cell.

What are the chances? Pretty remote? Yes, but if you if you add in the sheer vastness of space and throw millions of years into the mix then maybe not so incredible after all.

Did life (as we know it) start here or was it an import? Did planet earth get all the ingredients together or was life carried here on a meteor or comet, blown in on a solar wind or perhaps left here accidentally by some careless visitor millions of years ago. There could be altruistic creatures travelling around the various galaxies seeding suitable planets with life. Will they return one day to see how the crop is going? Will they be pleased or disappointed?

Of course, having living cells and throwing in time and thus evolution does not necessarily mean that any great or noble creature will emerge. I'm going to stick my neck out here and say that we humans are about the best effort so far. On earth anyway.

The giant reptiles were big and scary and modern-day creatures like lions and kangaroos are pretty interesting but us humans are about the only thing to date who show any long-term promise.

There are some humans who decry our species and broadcast their disgust at our less than wonderful track record. To them I say, don't give up on us we're an early prototype. We show a lot of potential. Besides, for comparisons you need a benchmark or standard. As far as I know we're the only game in town.

Of the other roughly 9 million species on earth, there are many who add greatly to the richness of life by their presence. Yes, a tiger will eat you but they are a very handsome beast. There are many that don't do much for their fellow creatures or the planet but then that is nature's way. Endless experimentation is what it's all about. Nearly every day creatures on this planet fade out of existence.

In many cases completely unnoticed. Are there others coming into existence? Yes. Evolution is a relatively slow process.

So life, this mysterious force within the simplest of living creatures through to the most advanced still presents a mystery to us all. We know what it is because we are aware of it and can define it. But why it is and what makes a collection of cells become animated and alive? That we don't entirely get.

Once again the marketing people from the various religions came up with a great little all-purpose answer. They invented the 'soul'. A handy generalised term for the spark that is life. They of course embellished it with various other properties including the possibility of selling said 'soul' to the enemy if you needed some ready cash or a favour.

I'm going to give them a 'free kick' here. Despite their ulterior motives they may by dumb chance be onto something. A 'soul' may not be all that far from the eventual truth. Not the handy religious soul that can be used by the various religious salespeople to help hook you into their particular brand of rambling dogma but the strange cross-over point, the spark, that starts the fire we know as life. What other as yet undiscovered, or noticed, properties might it hold. Perhaps life is a moveable, tradeable spark that can travel between dimensions and time and exist on various planes and in various forms.

There is so much we don't know. Our life journey has so far to go.

The Brain

The part of us that makes us the person we are ....

It's there in all living creatures. Admittedly in a very crude basic form in some but a control centre just the same, a place where the data is stored, information is received and dispatched, orders given, thoughts processed, plans made, lust managed ....
It's the brain. The part of us that makes us the person we are and how we see the world and the world sees us.
It could be argued that the bodies of creatures are nothing more than a transport and protection mechanism for the brain. (Though if this were entirely the case then a lot of brains would need to explain why they allow their bodies to do such stupid, risky, dangerous things when the destruction of the carrying mechanism would directly affect their own survival.)

The human brain is not a handsome organ. Made up of a lot of fat and water it looks like a great big lump of grey/pink waste material. Yet within its 40% grey matter (yes there really is grey matter) are 100 billion neurons that with help of the 60% of white matter, transmit and receive the signals that make the whole thing work. The brain has a serious need for blood and the oxygen it uses, taking about 20% of the body's supply. If the supply is cut off for just 10 seconds the person will lose consciousness.
Precisely 76% of our brains are comprised of the neocortex. Headquarters for everything if you like, though most of those who know about brains would probably vote the frontal lobe as their most interesting bit. It's where emotion, memory, language, problem-solving, sexual behaviour all hang out.
Those cognitive skills that give us a personality.
The brain is quite fragile but it is protected by floating in CSF and is encased in a quite robust bone container known as the skull.
In short, the brain is the essence of all that we are.

Like the hard disk in a computer new from the shop the brain comes with certain inbuilt features which allow it to function and perform many tasks related to survival and growth.
After that, it is open to downloads of information (software if you like) that it will use to form the character of the person in whom it is installed.
(NB Technologists predict that computers with a processing capacity matching the human brain are very close. Though having a capacity and how you use it

are two different things.
Will compassion or emotion play a part in the computers thinking? Enthusiasts suggest that AI without these burdens would make more rational decisions. Which in turn could lead to AI robots concluding that
humans are obsolete and no longer needed. We should think very carefully on that one.

How much the brain makes us who we are can be amply illustrated by a person with dementia. In the advanced stages of dementia, the sufferer loses all memory. The data they have collected and stored all their lives just seeps away until they are an empty shell with no awareness of who they are or where they are or the people around them. It is a heartbreaking time for spouses and those close to the person.
They are still alive, they look the same, they continue to exist but all the factors that made them the mother, father, aunt, brother etc are missing. It is possibly worse than the death of somebody with all faculties intact.
Death without the actual passing of the body.

One interesting dilemma the owners of a brain encounter is knowing if their brain is okay. Is it working as expected, to maximum capacity with all functions normal? The problem is fairly obvious, you're using your brain to assess your brain. Could it be leading you astray? Giving you false information? How do you find out? If you suspect your brain is plotting against you is this just a little light paranoia or are you insane?

Some say mental issues in the population can be as high as 20% but this ranges from major mental problems through to feeling a little anxious.
My best guess is, having assessed my own brain and compared myself to the people around me I think I'm fine. Nobody looks at me strangely, asks me if I'm okay, suggests I might need a rest or hints at medication. Besides, I think life is great and I'm having a good time living it.

Brain health is another form of physical health. In the world of affluent westerners obsessing about body shape and perfection, we have slightly lost the message that our brains need exercise as well. Let's not rush to make the gene pool shallower.

Knowledge, wisdom and mental power are the muscles of the brain. Like legs, arms, chest and hips the brain will serve you best when it's super fit.

It is here I must ask, "How are you and your brain getting on?"

And more importantly, "Are you happy with its performance?"

Most people will probably answer 'yes' because they have no ongoing issues with their life that can be directly blamed on their brain not doing its job.

We tend to blame other factors for not getting that promotion or winning the heart of some object of our desire.

Brains are like that, they keep a low profile and stay out of the way of controversy. A clever tactic in the complexities of life.

Perhaps next time you are not on top of your game it might be worth considering your brain's role in the downturn. Then consider what can be done about it. A stern talk, threats and punishment do not really cut it with brains. They will ignore you. The best approach is the subtle one. Plan to give your brain a bit of a boost. Some new information or better stimulation. A change of direction and some new goals. Even some healthier food. All these things make and keep brains happy.

In the end, you have to face the truth. You have been born and you have received your body. It was a package deal which included the latest model brain.

It is the only one you'll get. There are no refunds, changes of mind, try again, swapover, spare parts policies in place.

Accept and confront the situation. Make the most of it. Show it some respect. Try to get along.

Being on good terms with your brain can only be good for all concerned.

Time

Has it always been there ....

Time? Has it always been there?
The current time is 'now'. It always will be. As far as I know.
(What if I time travel? Well, your now will be wherever you are in time. There are thoughts that we could be in more than one place in time at once but that is a whole other book of possibles.)

"Time exists to stop everything happening at once." An enjoyable quote (which has been attributed to a number of sources) and may have a ring of truth about it. Consider time to be the filler that goes between all other events or matter. Everything exists within time. Of course, if we ever get off this planet and far enough away to experiment with the physical universe we may well find that time is anything but a rigid, ever-advancing clock and it is actually a quite flexible, fluid substance that can be manipulated, fiddled with and travelled about within.
Some argue that if time travel exists in the future then how come we've had no visitors. Possibly we have and we're just not very good at spotting them. Logically a smart traveller from the future would do some research and make an effort to go undetected.
Remember, all our experience, our knowledge, our conjectures and ideas are based on our existence on this one planet. The universe no doubt has surprises we could not even imagine. This is where time is our enemy. How do we get there? To the places in the universe where the laws of physics, dimensions, thought, reason, logic and time are open to new interpretations.

I have often looked at old photos. A street scene in a city back when photography had just been invented. What would it be like to step into that world, to walk down those streets, watch the people in their daily lives, look into shop windows? Could I purchase some item and transport it back to the present? Could I sit down for a meal in a cafe?
Many of us have had such thoughts. It can be more recent. Driving past a scene from our childhood and imagining ourselves back there occupying that space,

walking past an old shop or sitting under a tree in a park.

Time is a fascinating subject. Its existence seems obvious yet could it be possible to have a situation where time did not exist? Where the consequences of moving about within the walls that time has built around us were not an issue? Therein lies the paradox. Did we mistakenly invent/discover time and thus build those walls?

 Everybody knows the one about a tree falling in a forest. If it was not witnessed, how can we say it happened.

Was time always there and we just didn't notice it?

That child of chaos theory, 'The Butterfly Effect' is often quoted as a reason that even if time travel were possible, any interference in another time would have consequences, possibly catastrophic ones, therefore we should never travel in time.

The 'Butterfly Effect' has various forms but the most commonly quoted is that the flapping of the wings of a butterfly in an Amazon rainforest can be the start of a chain of invents that causes a

hurricane somewhere else on earth. It loosely relates to the dire warnings regarding moving about in time. Strict laws may apply for travellers.

Chaos Theory simply recognises that all actions have consequences. (Please no abuse for diluting Chaos Theory) It is the way the world is. We humans and all creatures interact with our environment. So do plants, chemicals, minerals and many other parts of our earth and universe. Yet we are still here. Making yourself a cup of tea at 3am or moving that pot plant from the front steps to the back porch may well bring about the destruction of space and time but it probably won't. Chaos theory doesn't stop at the earth it involves the whole universe. Out of chaos comes order? Balance? Patches of stability?

Getting back to everyday time. Those measuring devices like that clock on the wall, the wristwatch you wear, the digital number on your computer or phone. They all measure out our alloted time.

A time largely based on life cycles. They are ticking away our existence. They seem like an enemy because time cannot, will not, stop. Once again, as far as we currently know.

So on earth we live out our lives and we die. If we ever conquer space on a grand scale and find ways to navigate some of its massiveness then time will be right up there with speed, gravity, mental and physical health, as a wall we have to climb or defeat.

Imagine you could achieve or pass the speed of light and physically survive the impact. We'd still be travelling quite slow by space standards.

Of course, always being creatures who invent answers to impossible questions (eg Gods) we have imagined up wormholes. Litlle corridors that conveniently allow users to navigate to unreachable places by means of a convenient bend in space and time which allows us to pop through and out with no discernible health risks.

For now, time is with us and a part of us and our world. For the foreseeable future, it will sit like an annoying parrot on our shoulders interfering with our plans and limiting the space in which we can work.

Will humans exist long enough and evolve enough to break free? Hard to say. Certainly, we'll need to do a lot better than we have at the moment.

It may have to be a part of our existence whereby the nature of our lives is forced to change in order to accommodate ventures, travels and explorations which disrupt our previous normal by adding or subtracting great slabs of time. The basic family may give way to upgraded humans, produced in artificial wombs, who are born, given an implant and number and thus free of the old associations of brother, sister, father mother. Free to move on.

If we find time can be manipulated, cheated and used to our advantage, it is almost certain we humans, as is our nature, will exploit it.

Time will tell.

Death

You're going to die ....

Sooner or later in everybody's life, we come to accept that one day our life will end. It may come upon us in a sudden gut-wrenching moment or it may be a slow, subtle realisation of the fact. From the second we start life we have an appointment with its end. When my time comes I'll probably be saying, "No, no, wait. I haven't finished yet."
Death is cruel, it can come without warning in an accident, a mistake, a simple bit of rotten luck or fate. Some of us are born with a fault or defect that considerably shortens our lives. (Diversity within the human genome produces the variety we need for progressing the species but it gets it wrong quite a lot.) Then there is sickness, disease and probably the most prevalent cause of death being the vile, actions of others, through greed, ignorance, stupid beliefs and ideologies or plain hatred.

Unless someone can prove otherwise, we humans, like all things that attain life, have but one chance at 'living' and thus suffering its inevitable end.
Many, brave, courageous or perhaps foolhardy humans 'give up' their lives in conflict or to protect others or advance a cause in which they feel their demise is justified.
We seem to have created many more situations where we can end life than situations where life is preserved.

For the curious death is the last great experience. Though because of its nature, it does not allow the person having the experience to relay any useful information back to those who are yet to move onto the final phase. Perhaps there are many tips and observations that would be of great assistance to those experiencing death but so far communication from the departed has been nil. (Though we creative humans have of course invented many tales of those departed folk paying us visits. The only thing missing is any decent proof.)

I like the analogy of departing and asking for directions.
"Death? Why sure, it's just down the road aways, you can't miss it."

Many persons throughout history have sought an alternative to death ie 'the elixir of youth'.

Many a charlatan, schemer and ne'er do well has made good money by supplying said 'elixir.' The smart ones no doubt leaving town before the efficacy of their potion had been fully tested and found wanting.

When young, death is both scary and somehow heroic. To die young has a certain panache.

It is thought that in youth suicides the young person often sees the theatre that is their grieving friends, the words of sympathy and loss and their funeral at which they are the star, without fully comprehending that they will be dead and no longer part of this existence.

In later years nature seems to provide a drug-like acceptance of inevitable death. Older people talk of the calm and peace they feel as they get older. Obviously, nobody wants old people yelling, kicking and screaming about their plight. Dignity and stoicism is the order of the day.

The 'elixir of youth' salesmen still exist of course, their message has just been refined and given a marketing makeover.

From the crazily expensive face creams for women to the massive vitamin industry to the health clubs, spas, fitness trainers to cosmetic surgery to those seeking your spiritual longevity it's all business as usual.

In most cases, the perpetrators of these little money-making enterprises do not even have to skip town. Staying alive has become a self-obsessive occupation where none of the players of the game, actually believe in the game but they play it anyway.

I still wait in hope for the day when I switch on the evening news to find they're running a little puff piece about a very elderly person at their 102nd birthday party and the reporter sent to cover the event asks that traditional question, "Tell me, to what do you attribute your remarkable age."

The answer is usually something like "a cigar every morning and two shots of whisky every night," or "apple puree and vinegar four times a day."

Nobody ever gives the real answer.
"Good genes and heaps of very good luck."

A good death, if there is such a thing, is generally seen to be the person involved in the dying, lying peacefully in their bed at home, smiling contentedly at the assembly of sons and daughters, spouses, children and grandchildren all hovering near their bed, offering words of love and caring as they await the moment when their dear family member flickers out of existence with perhaps a gentle sigh.
The only thing that could make this scene more beautiful is the chance for the person about to depart to offer some quite profound utterance concerning love, life or the human condition just before they breathe their last.
The reality, of course, can blunt these ideals with less than perfect exits. Even if you do have a condition that allows a slow and reasonably dignified departure, it is highly likely that the event will take place in a hospital bed accompanied by a beeping machine that will indicate for all those present when the moment has come and gone.

Poet Dylan Thomas suggests -
Do not go gentle into that good night,
Old age should burn and rave at close of day;
Rage, rage against the dying of the light.

What can I say. If death offends you then by all means 'rage against the dying of the light'. If you're able, make your departure memorable. Fight this last great fight. You will lose as all those who have gone before have lost. But to leave death with a bloody nose is a satisfying final achievement.

The Past

Today is tommorow's past ....

The past is not some distant place. It is anything that has gone before. Today is tomorrow's past.

I was talking to a frail, elderly gent in a park a few years ago. He was quite candid about his limited future.

"Yep, I'm going to die soon but I've had a good run. More than many people."

He paused.

"There's one thing that makes me sad."

"What is that?" I asked.

"That when I go, all the memories, ideas, loves, thoughts, experiences, hopes and dreams I've had all disappear with me. That makes me sad."

This was an idea I had considered myself many times. I made me sad also.

As the past gets further away from the present it loses its detail, becomes more generalised and non-specific. Knowledge of a more distant past starts to group into loose slabs of history where decades, even centuries make little difference to the overall narrative.

Further back to an age and an earth, yet to be subjected to the dubious benefits of human habitation and we speak in aeons. Millions of years are tabled in graphs that give only tiny hints as to the exact happenings at the time. We use the skeletal remains of dinosaurs to illustrate great lumps of the earth's existence.

It is sobering to note that the dinosaurs who ceased to exist about 65 million years ago in the Cretaceous Period had been around for about 165 million years. (Note the casual use of the term millions of years.) Humans, even in our most basic form, can only be dated back to the Paleolithic Period. That's a mere 200 thousand years.

Will humans ever make it to even their first million years? The jury is divided on that one.

Interesting side note: Those creatures we know as Dinosaurs began, evolved, came and went in thousands of different species over their existence. If you revisited earth in say one million years from now you would no doubt find that

the human species we know has evolved into creatures we would not recognise. Either that or we're well and truly gone and perhaps an entirley different species of highly intelligent, sentient beings has evolved in our place.
That's the trouble with the present and the future, unlike the past they keep changing.

There's a well-worn phrase that says, "If you don't learn from the past (history) then you're doomed to repeat it."
Certainly with regards to the human obsession with aggression, war and horrible treatment of fellow humans that does seem to be the case. I'd imagine advanced beings visiting from another galaxy might find our behaviour quite contemptible. Although equally it could be argued that aggression equals survival and without it you won't get far in your galactic travels.
Putting that aside for the moment there is a lot of evidence that we continually learn from history and the past. Science and medicine, advances ever onwards based on the experimentations and ideas of those who went before.
Engineering, crop production, better ways of producing energy, safer ways of handling the world around us. All those good sensible lessons we have learned from the past mixed with our need to also produce better, more effective killing machines.

When the industrial revolution took place it was initially hailed as a new dawn for mankind. Factories sprang up to meet demand. Great technological leaps were made in methods, speed, efficiency and quality of the products produced, until somebody noticed that the atmosphere was becoming unbreathable and the streams and rivers undrinkable. The population was not benefitting at all from this new age. It was killing them.
We are still not fully cognisant of this lesson from the past. Nowadays poor countries forego their health and living standards in order produce goods for rich countries. Yet the pollution they produce still goes into the same atmosphere that we all breath and exist within.

Sometimes old ways prove to be the best ways. The past should not always be considered with a contemptuous sneer. Quite often we contemporary humans feel the need to 'improve' something that doesn't need improving because it already works perfectly well. There are many cases of us clever current generation humans having to quietly admit that the way they used to do it is just fine.

So going back to the beginning of this section, I repeat, "today is tomorrow's past." As we make our way through our allotted life span we are on a continuing treadmill creating a past on a daily basis. The easiest way to check this phenomenon is (for those of adulthood and a few years) to cast your mind back to your youth and teenage times. Consider what you admired back then as cutting edge technology and amazing science. Admit that many of those things are now laughable and/or embarrassing. Now that the marketing department has become involved in modern-day whiz-bang, can't live without, paraphernalia and profits are to be had, then the pace of change and a more compressed past is at hand.

Obsolescence is the new king. Items that had a lifespan of a decade or more are now superceded on a yearly basis. Such is the pressure for new, better models of everything that the past for a product could be last week. (It's why you can no longer buy many of those great candies and chocolates you enjoyed as a kid.)

If you're reading this text then logic suggests you are alive and functioning to some degree. If tomorrow a friend asks you what you did yesterday you will delve into your past and tell them you were reading this book called 'Lifeland.' You may even add that you found it 'wonderful' but that is not for me to judge.

When you die, as we all must, you will leave behind all your past and all those bits and pieces that made up the line of your life, will fade and splinter and be blown by the winds of time and simply cease to be. That's the past for you.

The Future

is all in front of you

When you are young, the future is all in front of you. When you age you still have a future and it's still in front, there's just less of it. Most people when they reach say 40 years old can remember a past that is different enough from their present to understand the many advances and benefits that have taken place in the brief future from their birth. (Perhaps they also recall some things that have changed and are now worse or have sadly ceased to exist.)

What of a serious future? Hundreds of years, thousands of years ahead. Wonderful, beautiful, free from disease? Utopia? Or a dark and miserable Distopia, ravaged by death and misery? A destroyed world.? We may have moved on. Left the wrecked remains of earth and populated other worlds. By our own hand in the manipulation of our DNA and by time itself we may have evolved into dozens of separate and different human species. Then again the human race may have run its course and gone the way of the dinosaurs.
We may no longer exist at all.
This question keeps hovering over all these discussions. Can/will humans survive long enough on earth to allow them to create the technology to escape from it? (Presumably with somewhere else to go.)

There's a great comedy line .... "how come I never see psychics winning Lotto or the Pools?"
One answer is because the future is not preordained, it is something we create as we move through each day. We arrive at the future each day and as we do we create more of it. Yes, a volcano erupting is not something we create but it is just nature's involvement in future creation.
Does this mean that if you jump in your time machine and head forward twenty years there will be nothing there because it hasn't been created yet? Hmmm, I wish I hadn't said that, because I really don't know. I suppose it depends on how and where you see time in the scheme of things. Are we it and there's nothing else or are we just a part of endless sets of realities. Is our whole existence already laid out like a story in a very large novel?

Conjecture like this only goes to prove how little we know about our circumstances and how far we are from any real concept of what it all means. It can be fascinating to sit with some fellow humans, get out some good whisky or wine and discuss all the possibilities but it can also be thoroughly depressing as the realisation of our ignorance seeps into the conversation. The most learned of us can still only make elaborate guesses about life, where we are, where our reality came from and the future of this universe.

I've noticed the more learned somebody is, the more conservative their list of possibilities. Those with less constrictions allow their minds to create all sorts of realities. From the hypothesis that we are simply experiencing this whole existence as a dream, to multiple or endless realities all occurring alongside each other, to our earth being a tiny part of some greater structure (this one works up or down in scale and brings up the interesting point that if we escape earth and spread we may turn out to be a cancer or virus in this greater being.)

One of the newer ones is that we are a breeding colony set out by greater beings in seeding the universe. A universe where millions of years are of no consequence.

Back to a future we can grasp. A future of possibilities and hope. As I write these words, the humans of this planet are finally noticing that their actions of late are causing the planet to make plans for their rejection Those folk who follow the GAIA principle (that the earth as a whole is a living thing) will be nodding their heads in agreement. Could it be that by endlessly and carelessly pumping waste into our atmosphere we are overheating the place to a point where life will cease. Then having shaken off this annoying parasite the earth will settle about rebuilding itself? Was Mars once like earth today?
Highly likely it was.

My attempt to break away from negative predictions didn't last a paragraph. For the sake of sanity I'd like to assume that we do create the future and we do have some say it how it will form, therefore sense will prevail, human spirit will overcome and our future will be generally okay.

I'd say if you're wondering whether to bother giving your children an inheritance or your grandchildren a few optimistic thoughts go right ahead.

It will then be up to you to make sure that this future you're busy creating is a good one.

One final thought.

We tend to see the future as always forging ahead, making bigger, better, longer, wider, greater versions of everything than before. Not so. For safety and common good, we may have to accept that we're not always able to accomplish these leaps ahead without 'consequences'. Being able to look at pieces of progress, analyse the consequences and sometimes walk away may be our greatest gift to a good future.

Nothing

There is always 'something' ......

Yes, the subject 'nothing' does not hold great promise for a fascinating end chapter in this book.

If you look in a dictionary for the word 'nothing' it says, 'no thing', 'not anything', 'naught'.

Yet 'nothing' represents our greatest puzzle.

The dictionary quite simply sums up the dilemma the human race has with our whole existence.

We live on a planet, in a world, where everything has a source, a beginning and an end. So when we look at this existence thing we ask that old question, "where did we come from?"

We don't have an answer. There's a lot of theories but no answer. Even if we had the answer it would lead to another question. "Where did where we come from, come from?" You can see where this is going.

The religious folk, of course, came up with God. (When in doubt about anything just throw in a god.)

If you ask them where God came from they will answer that he (she? it?) has always been. Okay, where did he get the materials to create the universe?

Well, they'll say, he brought them into existence.

It is pretty much is a continuous loop of silliness in which religion puts out these wonderful explanations but never any proof. They instead use the ultimate 'Catch 22' argument that you just need 'faith.' It is where all religion falls apart.

It does however raise the question we keep asking, "Can something be born of 'nothing'?"

Well, maybe it can. When Einstein suggested that space and time are free agents and we looked at spacetime as a 'fabric' it opened up a whole raft of new possibilities. With the previous restrictions on how we approached space and time lifted, black holes, multiples existences (multiverses) and all time existing at all time came up as subjects for serious discussion.

Once again, whatever is the answer or the multiple answers or the loop of continuity or the singularity of our purpose we still will ask, 'but where did it all

come from? Nothing?"
The concept that there was nothing and then slowly or rapidly (time did not yet exist) there was something, is beyond our levels of understanding. Still, we ask, "could it be so"?

On planet earth we cannot experiment with 'nothing' because there is always 'something' in the way. Whether there is a part of the universe that has a section of nothing I don't know. If it exists it could be argued that it is not nothing because it is part of the universe and thus it is part of something.
There are numerous theories doing the rounds of great minds. Some involve matter and antimatter.
Another is that 'nothing' is impossible and even in nothing there will be energy. The 'big bang' which seemed to have lots of fans is now losing traction as not the start of it all but simply a leap forward, a growth spurt if you like.
Anybody who looks at scans of living tissue and images of deep space might notice a certain similarity in the structure. This brings up the possibility of immense scales whereby universes can exist in areas that we would consider tiny while we may simply be the equivalent of a cell in a very, very large structure and the universe we see is just further parts of that structure.
Like so many things that we eventually understand, future humans may be highly amused by some of the current theories, as we are shocked at the ignorance of thinkers from our past but all questions have to be asked as we grope our way through existence.

In essence, we have these overriding questions. "Where and how did it all begin? From nothing?
If the answer is, "It has always been", then we need to rethink our whole concept of existence. Our little bit of knowledge gained while living on planet earth is just not enough.
If the answer is, "It started from nothing and here's the address where it happened", then we need to rethink our whole concept of existence. Our little

bit of knowledge gained while living on planet earth is just not enough. Although if the answer is the second one, then somebody is bound to ask, "What was there before?"

As a joke recently I suggested to a colleague that we start a theory of 'infinite disinterest'. In my theory, we humans are not capable of understanding the vastly complex machinations of existence and would be better served inventing ways to improve our health and happiness and finding a few spare earth-like planets. He didn't laugh. He rubbed his chin and said, "You may well have a point."

Would the answers, if ever found, prove how incredibly insignificant we are and throw us all into a bottomless malaise from which there was no escape?
Could it be we are seeking understanding that is beyond comprehension or is that just the talk of a defeatist?

I'm sure we'll not give up trying.

Why

It appears we exist. We are a bundle of cells that are programmed to turn into a human. We have one shot at existence. After that it's all conjecture.

Best to be getting on with whatever situation in which we find ourselves.
For some life will be good. It will be fulfilling and a life well-lived.
Others will have problems. Life will present challenges but with forbearance, it will turn out at least okay.
Others will have thoroughly miserable lives full of terrible events, suffering and heartache.
It is simply the way it is.
There are too many factors involved in how and at what time we begin and finish our lives.
Hundreds of years ago life was much shorter and there was a lot less chance of happiness. In the future, there may be chances of longer life but happiness is not guaranteed.

My advice is -
Come what may, we only get one brief chance at life, so do what you can to make it work. Enjoy as much as you're able. You can be a bit selfish.
You cannot treat every day as if it were gold because existing has mundane parts to it that require your attention.
However, you can plan 'special' days. Pick a day a few weeks ahead, choose something a little extraordinary to do. Alone or with others. It may not always work but there will be some 'special' days that will stay with you till your last breath.

As long as you have life -
Use it!

How

So you have this thing called 'life'.
You can tell you're alive because you are aware. (Medically you can be alive and unaware but we'll put that aside for now.)
What do you do with this 'life?'
Yes, eat, sleep, love, procreate and so on ……. but what else?
Well, try giving something. It could be minor or quite major. Whatever is within your capacity. Build, change, improve an aspect of existence that will survive after you have gone.
No, I don't suggest a shiny new barbecue area in the yard, I want something that has meaning.

On a beach headland I know, I found a nice, well-constructed concrete armchair. One that will last a long time against the elements. It was facing the beach and ocean. A local man who had given so much to the community had died. Another local man who only knew the dead man by sight and reputation had noticed that he came down to the headland most days and sat looking at the ocean. Perhaps it brought him peace. So this stranger built the dead man a decent seat so others would have somewhere to sit and perhaps find peace. He added a plaque in memory of the dead man and asked that the local council forgive him for not submitting a planning application. They did.

Maybe concrete seats are not your thing. That's okay. Give it some thought. Physical, mental, astronomical or tiny.
Just something that will last.
You'll feel good. Trust me. You don't even have to take credit.
Secret deeds are the most enriching.

Look for a need - Fulfil it!

Where

If you live in a war-ravaged country devoid of all decency and hope then my heart goes out to you. Unfortunately, the world is an imperfect place. From my rather privileged western background, I can only look and feel for your suffering. There is a limit to what I, or we, can do.
Where you are born, where you live and how you live are often determined by fate, (whatever fate is) and the people around you.
Thus your destiny may be predetermined and all the wit and wisdom you apply may not be enough.

Apply what you have - Don't be sad!

For those of us who are in a good place don't ask 'where' just do it.

Other

This whole work came about by accident. I was holding onto my phone in my office waiting for the person at the other end to find some information I needed. It was taking a while. I began to scribble down thoughts onto a notepad. Subject headings for an imaginary book about life.
The subjects were random. Whatever came into my head I wrote down. When the phone conversation ended I looked at my notepad and thought maybe I should go ahead and actually write this book.
The subjects I had scribbled down were rather odd. Dogs? Wine? Chocolate and Bread? Life, Death and so on? What was I thinking?
The temptation was to change the list to some more conventional, less difficult subjects but then I decided that if my mind came up with this challenge then I should accept it and see what came out of it all.

So here is the result.
Have I got the balance right or is this whole book just a self-indulgent lot of rambling?
Of course, it is.
That's what I like about it. Whatever came to mind I wrote it down.
No editing, updating, changing to a more pleasing prose that would stroke the reader's ego and feed their id. It's repetitious and flawed.
(A human condition.)
What you see is what you get.

Which brings me to the point of telling you this.
For all of us, there will be only a few rare moments in our life where we briefly let go or are temporarily taken out of our carefully constructed and very extensive comfort zone.
These moments may not be immediately recogniseable but they will happen.
What we do with them is the interesting part of the puzzle.

For the majority, we will reject them and retreat to our safe, secure way of life in which no influence could lead us toward anything that is not completely comfortable. Keep in mind I am not talking about physical challenges such as being scared of heights then deciding to skydive. The challenges I suggest will be more cerebral.

Don't be disillusioned if you recognise one of these events and decide to stay safe. I offer no guarantee that by going down this 'road less travelled' you will be enlightened, a better person or happy with the outcome.
It is the taking of the chance that is the 'interesting' part of the exercise. The outcome is almost irrelevant

NB There are blank pages and spaces between many subjects in this book. They are there for you to add your own views, arguments, notes, private praise of the author or just to doodle some meaningless but enjoyable words or illustrations. That way this book will be unique and be your own.

Who is James Caspet anyway?

Recognise moments -
Consider your response!

What to worry about

Why to not

Paths to take

Places to Avoid

Exercises

AND FINALLY
Thoughts, ideas and questions

What to worry about

Worry is part of the human condition. If you're concerned that you worry too much it may be because you worry too much.

What we humans do know is that, on our time scale, the end of everything is not next week.

So ...... make a list. Make several lists if necessary of all your worries.

It is very therapeutic. When you make a list you're transferring at least a little (sometimes a lot) of your concerns onto the piece of paper. "Yes, I'm concerned about .... but now it's on the list.

Now for the good bit. Make another list. Call it the A List if you like. Grab a cup of your favorite beverage. (Hot is better.)

Then go through your other list/s and be hyper-selective, ruthless. Choose only the items that are of great and immediate need and are achievable.

Put them on your A List.

The maximum number on your A List should be ten or less. (Any more and you've started worrying again.)

Take your other list/s and put them somewhere out of sight and out of mind.

Do not go near or think about the other list/s.

Sort out, solve or dismiss all the things on your A List. Take your time.

Then and only then you may consult your other list/s. You will almost certainly find that a lot of the items shown on your other list/s have gone away, become unimportant or have solved themselves.

Why to not

Because it will not fix the problem that worries you.

Paths to Take

From the moment we are born, in fact, before we are born, decisions are being made. Who become your parents? What situation you are born into? What care is going to be taken of you once you are born?

Then you are there. You exist. From then on you are making decisions.

Very minor ones at first. To cry or not to cry etc.

As you grow your ability to make decisions and the level of their consequence increases to a point where the path you take is entirely your choice.

Here is where your life, how you spend it and what becomes of you and all those with whom you interact reaches new heights of importance. Yet it's mostly arbitrary. None of us will make all of life's decisions wisely or for the best outcomes. Some will be just dumb, emotional decisions while others will be irrational but for perhaps noble reasons such as love or honour or for a greater good. You can't avoid them. (You chose to read this book.)

We can often recognise good or bad decisions after they are made but rarely before they are made. Some we may not even notice as having a profound influence on our life and its outcomes.

All our life we have to make decisions. They happen many times a minute.

They're part of life. Very few are momentous. Being sidetracked by some household chore means you leave to go shopping slightly later and thus change the outcome of a traffic accident several suburbs away. You'll never know. Mostly the decisions you and everyone around make just mean life goes on.

Here's a list of path taking considerations for big decisions-
1. Will this be a risk and is the risk acceptable?
2. Will this bring harm or good to anyone including me?
3. Am I scared or relaxed?
4. Will I know or care if it was the right decision?
5. Consider your life a year, a decade later, based on this decision.

Places to Avoid

Of course, there is that bad neighbourhood, the bar with an unsavoury reputation and the guy who can get you just about anything you want if you have the price.

Life also has places to avoid. They are to do with more subtle choices, often almost subconscious reflexes when the mind you have used all your life has to see you right and not let you down.
If you started early and developed the resources at your disposal, your mind's instincts should keep steering you with some degree of innate wisdom.

Should you be reading this section waiting for the 'list' of places to avoid then you are to be disappointed. The list would be too long, too complex and open to variation and interpretation.
It is mind training you need and no matter how good your mind becomes it will, on occasions, let you down. Survive the experience and your mind will be even more acute and aware.
What you approach and experience when young may be something you avoid in later years. Is this acquired wisdom, caution or cowardice? Either way, it is probably correct.
Mind programming is a lifelong pursuit. Each day adds to the inventory. Each day may increase or decrease the best results but overall age brings greater power to steer a path best suited to your wishes and hopes.
There will never be a day in your life where your acquired skills will unfailingly keep you away from places to avoid but you can come quite close to perfection.

For those who are thinking that this page and the last are about the same thing. They're not. Paths to Take are conscious or near conscious decisions whereas Places to Avoid comes down to instinct.

Exercises

Find a dog in a relaxed mood and have a chat.

Go far enough into a forest to be completely alone then just listen.

On a clear night go into the country far from city lights, lay in a field and look up.

Learn to appreciate good wine for the taste. Do not brag about it.

Learn enough of a language then go to that country and have a conversation.

Cook something that you would not normally dare to try.

Ask your friends the meaning of it all. Watch their faces.

On a cool, sunny day walk out your gate and keep walking straight for an hour.

Find something good about somebody you dislike. (May not work but try.)

Find something negative about somebody you admire. (May not work but try.)

See how many times you can breath in with no out.

Buy a powerful magnifying glass and take another look at your world.

Sit alone and silent in a room for a day.

Stay long enough in a foreign land to get to know the local people.

Make a list of the things that are common to all humans.

Make a list of things that are common to all mammals.

Make a list of things that are common to all life.

Force yourself into another world. Notice small things. (Not necessarily tiny.)

Find somebody else who has read this book. Discuss. (Not argue.)

Stand on a crowded street corner and make a list of 10 uplifting people moments.

Record yourself reading your favourite poem. Listen back at high volume. Do more.

Sing. It's very uplifting. (You'll sound odd at first but confidence will grow.)

Make a movie of yourself talking about life. Playback, listen to what you said.

Volunteer in some group or organisation that does good things. (Avoid religious.)

If you've volunteered for many years maybe stop. Move on.

Think of a profound statement that will take hold in human vernacular.

Count your blessings. Do a recount. What is a blessing anyway?

Do you have friends or just acquaintances? Consider.

Company person or person who works for a company? Consider your decision.

If you met yourself in the local park what would you talk about.

Put on some music and dance for 15 minutes non-stop.

Find a silent, pitch black room. Insert ear plugs. Sit and think for an hour.

Do the above for three hours. (How will you know the time? Count? Guess?)

Consider friends who refuse to recognise/discuss difficult subjects. Move on?

If any of these exercises make you uncomfortable, that's more reason to participate.

Thoughts, ideas and questions

We always see more looking back.
Really good actors aren't acting.
A boy needs a dog. Does a dog need a boy?
Knowing when to leave is as important as staying.
One of the consoling factors in being paranoid is that 50% of the time you're right.
Time chooses us.
We invented time so that we could be aware of not standing still.
Eagles high up look like falling leaves.
A tiny light in a darkened room seems very bright.
What if the dark in a dark corridor did not end?
When you're old you give hugs but don't recieve any.
Appreciation of life increases as it runs out.
Being young is temporary. So is being old apparently.
History is replete with men with silly moustaches.
One day you stop saying "I love you." Only years later do you notice.
Democracy is the best we have. Its fault is that anybody can vote. Discuss.
Keep kicking a dog and it will bite you - or it will simply leave.
Life is a work in progress. Its completion date is someway off.
Compliments from fools should not be taken out of context.
You cannot explain to a mad person that they are mad.
Your freedom is relative to the freedom of others.
No child knows their parents as a child.
The acquisition of money has never given anybody good taste, civility or greater intelligence.
Minorities and committees dilute the world.
Analysing life is all I have so far ....
Time doesn't heal, it allows fading.
An important reason for Government Departments is to employ the unemployable.
I have reached a stage of my life where I'm seeking to buy time. It is very difficult to purchase.

Actors are always acting. At times they use a script.

Sadly the creative endeavours of those with talent are judged by those with none.

Asking for advice creates much more noise than asking for help.

Is life a compromise for what could be had at greater risk?

A long time ago is yesterday in your memory.

If you hold time in your hand and squeeze hard, when you open your hand it will be empty.

Why do vegans try so hard to create vegetable copies of the foods they loath?

Do plants suffer when they are harvested?

Every moment happens only once. (Notwithstanding alternative realities of course.)

A perfect poem is a rare thing.

Why do we so often try to answer questions for which we have no answer?

I've been to the future - it isn't there.

Most dreams are disturbing at best so why the term, 'A Dream Come True.'

Do Vegans realise that the animals they wish to save would not exist if we were all vegans?

Imagine if reproduction required three parties to participate.

So many things to do and only one lifetime.

Life is a series of choices. It's like sailing the ocean with no compass.

In a world where shallow is the norm, seek some depth.

Nobody remembers the fashionable.

Not enough rain and we die. Too much rain and we drown.

The answer lies between any two extremes.

Truth should be used sparingly in conversation, it tends to upset people.

Science moves forward. Religion does not.

Isn't it refreshing to sometimes meet an 'expert' who can say, "I don't know."

Some great things are born of mistakes.

Problems have many doors. Leave by one and enter by another.

Would those with six fingers play better piano?

Listen to 2year-olds. They haven't learnt to conform.

Consider your life if one of your senses was lost.

What could a sixth sense be?

Nobody knows everything. Knowledge is relative.

Wilderness helps you appreciate civilisation. Stay longer and appreciate the wilderness.

Good vintage cheese makes your gums itch.

Good food is nice but have we gone too far into ridiculous?

Are businesses mission statements meant to be funny?

Smart is often realworld dumb.

It is rare that there is one right answer.

Don't question everything. Develop the knack of picking those that need examination.

Boys are boys. Daughters are different.

Books are comfortable. Tactile and friendly.

A room with bookshelves is complete.

Mobile/Cell phones are not your entire life. Look up, walk away.

Experts tend to have more answers than the question deserves.

Imagine if you knew everything.

Being right is good. Being wrong is learning.

Which part of the world makes you comfortable?

If you relived a great moment in your life, would it still be great?

Are we the alpha species or do we just think we are?

Could we be devolving?

I like to think. Some people don't.

If there is an end to everything, what's next?

You need positive and negative for the current to flow.

A brain needs a body and a body needs a brain. It's the balance that counts.

I could keep going here but I've decided to stop. (See next page.)

Your thoughts, ideas and questions

Date _____ Write one word that describes your life.	Date _____ Three weeks later. Write three words that describes your life.
Date _____ Three months later. Write six words that describes your life.	Date _____ One year later. Write twelve words that describes your life.

I invented this simple little timeline for those who want to explore their life.
There's no right or wrong answers.
Though if you wrote 'perfect' in the first box you're rare and lucky or in denial.
If you wrote 'interesting' then you have something to explore.
If you wrote 'horrible' then you have something to work on you're just hard to please.

Don't get carried away. Leaving your wife and children and heading off to live on a mountain while examining your navel is not life-changing it's just self-indulgent and completely missing the point. Doing something that enriches you and those around you. That has merit.

How to end? Perhaps with a story.

As a young man, I lived for some years in London. In the early days, I shared a flat with some Brits. One Saturday morning we went to the markets nearby. In an idle moment, we bought a small cactus.

Upon returning to the flat and after some drinking had taken place we decided our new cactus needed a name. Arguments regarding the name raged back and forth for some time. Finally, after a quite exhausting session, one of the Brits stood and proclaimed,

"That's it. No more. It's 'Spikey', full stop!"

In the brief silence that followed, I said,

"No, that's not quite it. It should be 'Fikey Spullstop.'

And so it came to pass.

'Fikey Spullstop' spent a brief but happy life in our abode till sadly he passed away from neglect. Mixed with my guilt I do like to think that the little cactus overcame the lack of attention shown to him by being very proud of his unusual name.

From little moments to major. Think a little more. Move outside the obvious.

Go that extra step.

(How do I know it was a male cactus? I don't.)

Note Pages

Be thoughtful rather than aggressive

Note Pages

Be brave rather than careless

Note Pages

Be enlightened rather than critical

Note Pages

Use pencil (Some notes may require editing.)

www.ingramcontent.com/pod-product-compliance
Lightning Source LLC
Chambersburg PA
CBHW081230080526
44587CB00022B/3886